All of us have heard about comets, those huge dirty snowballs with long tails. And meteors, the "falling stars" so commonly sought after on hot summer nights. Even asteroids, similar to meteors, but larger and farther out in space, are familiar objects.

For centuries we have enjoyed viewing these bodies and marveling at them, while only guessing at what they really are. In text and photos, Melvin Berger probes deeply into the composition and complexities of these awesome objects, bringing to light the significant research and discoveries of ancient and modern astronomy.

What are too casually called just "debris in the sky," comets, meteors and asteroids are now unfolding for us a spectacular glimpse of the universe and bringing us closer and closer to unlocking the mysteries of our vast and wondrous solar system.

Comets, Meteors and Asteroids

by Melvin Berger

G. P. Putnam's Sons/New York

For Gilda, with all my love

Photo Credits
American Meteorite Laboratory: pp. 38, 40 (right), 54   Celestron International: Cover, pp. 2, 23,
32   Hale Observatories: pp. 21, 31   Harvard College Observatory: pp. 42, 63   Institute of Meteoritics, University of New Mexico: p. 52   Mount Wilson and Palomar Observatories: p. 6   NASA: pp.
9, 13, 18, 34, 37, 68   Smithsonian Astrophysical Observatory: pp. 40 (left), 46   U.S. Naval
Observatory: pp. 14, 50   Diagrams on pp. 12 and 60 and drawing on p. 66 by Yehuda A. Cohen

Library of Congress Cataloging in Publication Data
Berger, Melvin.   Comets, meteors and asteroids. Includes index.   Summary: Discusses the char-
acteristics of comets, meteors and asteroids, their relationship to and effects on the earth, and what
they reveal about the history of the universe.   1. Comets—Juvenile literature. 2. Meteors—Juvenile
literature. 3. Planets, Minor—Juvenile literature. [1. Comets. 2. Meteors. 3. Planets, Minor]
I. Title.   QB721.4.B47   523.6   80-39720   ISBN 0-399-61148-7

Contents

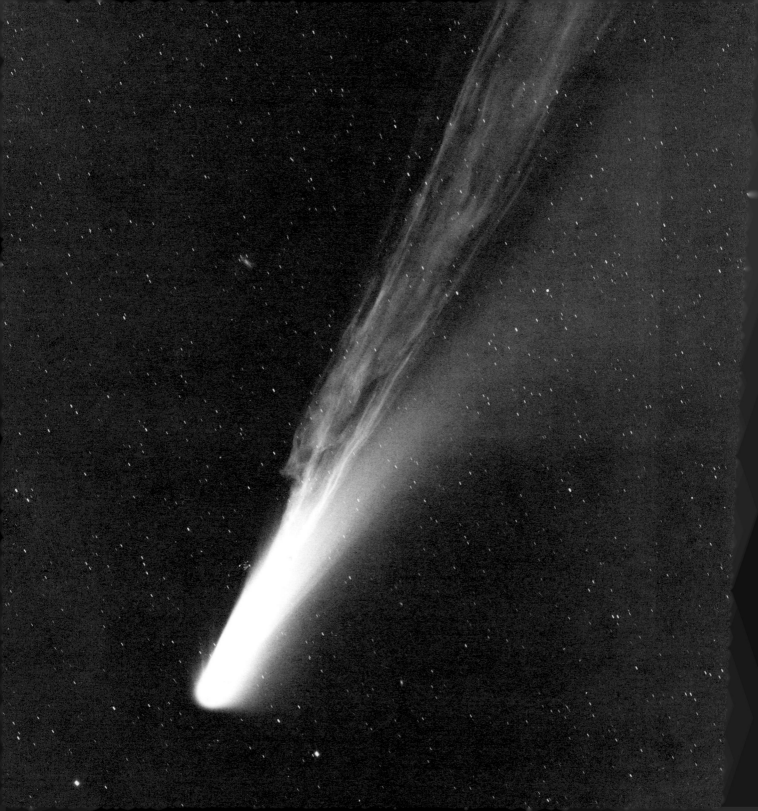

1/ Debris in the Sky

Brilliant comets flash across the heavens. Huge meteors burst into view, casting their light over entire countries. Showers of sparkling meteorites cascade down to earth like heavy snowfalls. Giant asteroids pass dangerously close to the planet earth.

These strange and fascinating objects exist within our solar system: comets, bodies of ice containing bits of solid matter and looking like immense dirty snowballs; meteors, stone and metal objects that range in size from tiny grains to huge boulders; and asteroids, solid bodies similar to meteors but larger, some reaching the size of small planets.

People have long viewed these heavenly bodies—and their visits to earth—with wonder and awe. To our ancestors, a comet or meteor streaking across the sky was a message from God. It was an announcement of some great event that was about to occur. The Bible tells us that a comet lit up the sky when Jesus Christ was born. A hail of meteorites destroyed Joshua's enemies in battle.

More recently, some eight thousand square miles (102,000 sq. km) of forest in Siberia were destroyed by an object from outer space. A woman in Alabama was struck on the leg by an eight-and-one-half-pound (3.9 kg) stone that fell from the sky. In 1973, a religious group proclaimed that the appearance of the Kohoutek Comet signaled the downfall of the United States.

Billions of comets, meteors and asteroids are in flight throughout the solar system. They share the space with the sun and the nine planets.

The sun is a star, a huge ball of superhot gas. Heat and light energy pour out of the sun making life on earth possible.

The earth is one of a group of four similar planets. All are solid bodies made up mostly of rock and metal. Because they are somewhat alike, we call these planets the earthlike, or terrestrial, planets. In order of their distance from the sun, they are Mercury, Venus, Earth and Mars.

From Mars to the next planet, Jupiter, there is a wide gap of about 340 million miles (547 million km). Jupiter, Saturn, Uranus and Neptune make up the major, or Jovian planets. (They are sometimes called Jovian planets since Jove is another name for the god Jupiter.) These planets are much larger than the terrestrial planets. Rather than being made of solid material, they are composed of gases, mostly hydrogen and helium. Pluto, the planet most distant from the sun, is sometimes classified with the major planets, even though it is different from them in many ways.

Think of the planets as a group of houses at a building site, and the comets, meteors and asteroids as the debris, the material left over after construction. They are the stone and metal pieces that remained after the planets were formed nearly five billion years ago.

Suppose you examine the debris around the building site and find stone slabs and steel beams. You would guess that these materials were used in the construction and can be found inside the houses. You might even be able to figure out how the different materials were put together to erect the structures.

Scientists study comets, meteors and asteroids in the same way. They try to learn more about these objects, both to understand the objects themselves better and to discover more about the planets of

Large numbers of objects from space land on earth every day. This meteorite landed in Antarctica in 1978.

the solar system and how they came into being.

Few of us today believe, as our ancestors did, that comets, meteors and asteroids are messages from God. But we cannot help but be fascinated by these mysterious, heavenly bodies. Great numbers of them land on earth every day, sometimes causing widespread destruction. Others pass close enough to earth to produce spectacular displays in the sky and to threaten devastating collisions. There is always the possibility that, someday, one may completely change the face of our planet.

Comets, meteors and asteroids are interesting of and by themselves. They affect our lives in ways that we know and in ways we are yet to discover. But, above all, they give all of us a glimpse of our universe at a time in the far distant past when it was quite different from the way it is today.

2/ Comets

A Dirty Ice Ball

A well-known astronomer once described a comet as a "dirty ice ball." This is not exactly a scientific description, but it does give a basic idea of a comet's makeup.

The solid center, or nucleus, of a comet is made mostly of ices. The ices are mainly frozen water, ammonia, methane and carbon dioxide. Trapped in this ball of ice is dirt, bits of rock and metal.

Picture a scoop of chocolate-chip ice cream. The scoop of ice cream is like the frozen ice of the nucleus. The chocolate chips are like the rock and metal bits that are scattered throughout. The nuclei (plural of nucleus) of most comets are between one half mile (0.8 km) and thirty miles (50 km) in diameter. The dirt bits range in size from tiny grains to walnut-sized lumps.

Surrounding the nucleus is the coma. It is not solid like the nucleus; rather, it is made up of gases and dust that extend out from the nucleus. It usually has a diameter of up to 625,000 miles (1 million km).

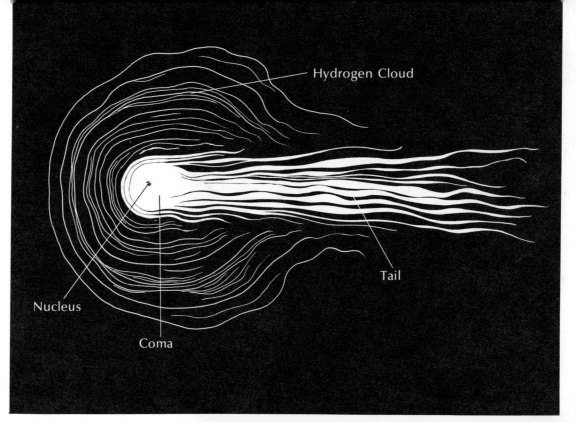

Hydrogen Cloud

Tail

Nucleus

Coma

(above) Parts of a comet (right)
*The elliptical orbit of a comet
around the sun.*

Sun

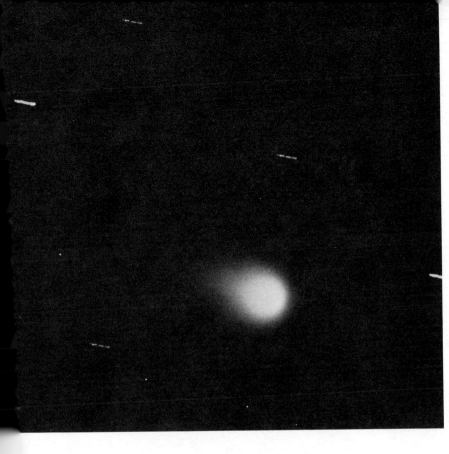

The nucleus of a comet is a ball of ice with bits of rock and metal frozen inside.

The Great Comet of 1811 had the biggest coma ever recorded. It was 1.25 million miles (2 million km) across its widest point.

Together the nucleus and the coma make up the head of the comet.

Bagful of Nothing

The head of the comet is followed by the tail, which has been jokingly referred to as a "bagful of nothing." Like the coma, the tail is made mostly of gases, with some dust mixed in. Unlike the coma, it is straight, narrow and rather streamlined in shape.

The molecules of gas in the tail are much farther apart than those in

the coma. The gas is very thinly spread out—so thinly spread out that one cubic inch (16.4 cc) of the air surrounding the earth contains more gas molecules than 21 million cubic yards (16 million ckm) of a comet's tail!

The gases themselves are different, too. Those in the tail are ionized; that is, some electrons have been stripped away from the molecules. Molecules are balanced collections of positive and negative particles. Since electrons are charges of negative electricity, their loss leaves the gas molecules with a positive charge. Any molecule with a charge, either positive or negative, is called an ion.

The sun creates both the coma and the ionized gas in the tail. First, heat and radiation from the sun melt and vaporize the solid ices of the comet's nucleus. They change the solid material into gas. The gas molecules and the dirt particles that were trapped in the ices form the coma.

The sun also emits a high-speed stream of subatomic particles, known as the solar wind. The solar wind pushes on the gas molecules and dust particles in the coma. It spreads them out to form the comet's long tail. This same solar wind strips the electrons from the gas molecules in the tail, creating the ions.

The coma and the gas tail usually develop as the comet comes rather close to the sun. They appear when the comet is within two Astronomical Units of the sun. One Astronomical Unit, or AU, equals 93 million miles (150 million km). This is the average distance between the sun and the earth. Thus, the sun's radiation and the solar wind create the coma and tail when the comet comes within 186 million miles (300 million km) of the sun.

15

The solar wind creates the tail that flashes out from the head of the comet.

This old print shows the Great Comet of 1843, which had a tail estimated to be 200 million miles.

Because the tail is created by the pressure of the solar wind on the head of the comet, it always faces away from the sun. This looks natural when the comet is heading toward the sun, but when the comet is moving away from the sun it looks very strange. The tail is actually in front of the head of the comet.

Compare the comet's tail with the smoky exhaust of a fast-moving car. The car's smoke trail always extends out behind the car, no matter which direction it is traveling. The comet's tail, though, extends out behind the comet only when it is going toward the sun. At other times the tail is either ahead of, or to the side of, the comet.

The Great Comet of 1843 had the longest gas tail of any comet ever seen. It is estimated to have been 200 million miles (320 million km) in length.

Some comets have more than one tail. The second tail is frequently curved and wide. Mostly it is made up of tiny bits of dust from the comet's nucleus. It may be as long as the gas tail. And like the gas tail, it always faces away from the sun.

The head and part of the tail of the comet are enveloped in a giant cloud of hydrogen gas. The first hydrogen clouds were discovered around 1970 by two spacecraft, the Orbiting Astronomical Observatory 2 and the Orbiting Geophysical Observatory 5. They were launched in 1968 on a research mission by the National Aeronautics and Space Administration (NASA). One of their purposes was to study comets. The craft found two comets surrounded by hydrogen clouds that were millions of miles wide. Other observations since then have helped astronomers realize that the hydrogen cloud is as much a part of a comet as the nucleus, coma, gas tail and dust tail.

The hydrogen clouds that surround comets were discovered with this spacecraft, the Orbiting Geophysical Observatory 5.

Viewing Comets

The entire length of a comet, from the edge of the hydrogen cloud to the end of the tail, stretches across a vast section of the sky. Yet comets actually contain very little mass or matter. How do scientists know this?

Most of our knowledge of comets comes from indirect evidence. By careful study of the orbits of various comets, we know that our planet earth has passed directly through the tails of comets at least twice. At the times of these passings, though, there was no tangible evidence to show that we were traveling through anything but the emptiness of space. This is because the matter that makes up the comet is so thinly spread out it cannot be detected.

Also, comets sometimes pass in front of the sun, or between the earth and the stars. Astronomers have never been able to detect any measurable drop in light from the sun or stars during these passes. This is another indication that the comet is not very dense.

On the few occasions when comets did come somewhat near the earth, they did not alter the earth's orbit. If comets had great mass, the attraction of their gravity would have changed the earth's path through space.

Some of what is known about comets does come from direct observation through a telescope. A telescope is an optical instrument that aids the human eye in seeing distant objects, such as planets or stars.

Comets produce their light in two ways. Some of it is reflected sunlight that bounces off the dust particles in the comet. The yellowish color of the dust tail, for instance, comes from the reflected sunlight. Added light comes from the fluorescence of the ionized molecules in the gas tail. As radiant energy from the sun knocks electrons from the gas molecules, other electrons replace the missing ones, and in doing so produce tiny bursts of light. As this happens in all of the ionized molecules, it gives the comet a bright, bluish light.

The comet's light also lets the astronomers learn about the chemical makeup of the comet. They aim their telescopes at the comet, and pass the light into a device called a spectroscope. In the spectroscope the light goes through a glass prism that splits the light beam into a rainbowlike band of colors, referred to as the strip.

A number of dark lines appear in a pattern along the strip. These lines are created by the various atoms and molecules in the comet. Each chemical creates its own particular dark lines. The location of the lines indicates exactly which chemicals are present. Study of these lines reveals the chemical compounds that make up the ices and shows the presence of rock and metal bits in the nucleus. And it points up whether or not the gas-tail molecules in the comets are ionized.

Comets in Space

Most comets move in orbits around the sun, much as planets do. By making a number of observations, astronomers are able to plot the entire orbit of a comet, and then, by means of this orbit, recognize the comet when it nears the earth again.

Comets' orbits around the sun are known as ellipses. An ellipse is a curve traced around two points. If the two points are close together, the ellipse is round, almost like a circle. If the two points are far apart, the ellipse is shaped more like the outline of a cigar.

The planets' ellipses around the sun are rounded and circlelike. Comets' ellipses are much more elongated or cigarlike.

Some of the light of a comet is reflected sunlight.

You can draw both kinds of ellipses in a simple experiment. Tack a blank sheet of notebook paper onto a bulletin board. Push two more thumb tacks partway into the paper near the center and about two inches (50 mm) apart. Tie a string loosely from tack to tack. Let the string sag in the middle.

Now place a pencil inside the string. Swing the pencil around in all directions. The curve you trace will resemble the circlelike orbit of the planets.

Remove the two center tacks and place them twice as far apart. Leave about four inches (102 mm) between them. Connect the tacks with the same string as before and trace a curve. Notice how the ellipse is more elongated with rounded ends. It approximates the cigar-shaped orbit of the comet.

Comets vary according to the length of time it takes them to make a complete orbit. This length of time is called the period. About three out of every four comets have long periods. They take from hundreds to millions of years to make one complete orbit. Their journey takes them from near the sun to the outermost limits of the solar system.

The long-period comets are usually very bright. They reflect a great deal of light because they have a substantial amount of material in the nucleus. Since they have passed the sun only a few times, very little of the nucleus has been vaporized. The larger the nucleus, the brighter the comet.

The short-period comets have periods of 3.3 to perhaps 200 years. These comets have made many fly-bys around the sun. Every time they pass the sun they lose a good deal of gas and dust. Eventually, because they have passed the sun so frequently, they lose all their material, fall

Comets move in vast orbits through the skies.

apart, and disintegrate. Because of this, a number of short-period comets observed over past centuries can no longer be seen.

Hints from History

Comets have always been linked to major events on earth, usually unfavorable ones. Even after the first astronomers worked out the movements of the stars and planets in the skies, they wondered about the unpredictable and unexpected appearance of comets. These early investigators of space thought of comets as strange, and probably foreboding, stars. And since it was widely accepted that stars controlled, or at least influenced, the affairs of humans, comets were considered bad omens.

Major events are occurring on earth all the time. Therefore, the appearance of a comet can almost always be connected to some evil or dire happening. The murder of Julius Caesar in 44 B.C. occurred at nearly the same time a bright comet appeared in the sky. Shakespeare noted this coincidence in his play *Julius Caesar.* But he was also quick to point out: "When beggars die, there are no comets seen."

No one is quite sure which comet was seen in 44 B.C. But most of the future sightings have been of a comet we know as Halley's Comet. (It is pronounced to rhyme with "rally," not "daily.") This comet is one of the brightest in the sky. It returns approximately every 76 years, giving it one of the longest orbits of the short-period comets.

Halley's Comet passed by the earth in 11 B.C. Some say that it is this comet, in fact, that was called the Star of Bethlehem, and is associated with the birth of Jesus Christ. Giotto's painting, *Adoration of the Magi,* shows the comet in the sky above the stable where the infant Jesus

Giotto's painting "Adoration of the Magi" shows Halley's comet in the sky at the time of the birth of Jesus Christ.

was born. The comet was known to Giotto because it also appeared in 1301, two years before the artist started work on his painting.

The same comet was visible in the year 1066 when William the Conqueror invaded England from France, as illustrated in the Bayeux tapestry. During its 1456 appearance, Pope Calixtus III placed a curse on the comet because of the growing belief that comets were agents of the devil. Two centuries later, in 1681, the town council of Baden, Switzerland, frightened by another sighting of the comet, ordered

ISTI MIRANT STELLA

HAROLD

The 11th century Bayeux tapestry has Halley's comet in the top center. It illustrates the appearance of the comet in 1066 when the Normans defeated King Harold of England.

everyone to attend mass and sermon every Sunday and feast day.

The noted American author Mark Twain was born in 1835, the year Halley's Comet made another appearance. Twain predicted that his death would occur during the year of the comet's next visit in 1910.

The fact is that he did die that very same year. As Twain put it, "I came in with the comet, and I will go out with the comet."

Probing the Mysteries

The ancient Greeks were the first to try to learn more about comets. They named these bodies *aster kometes,* which means "star with long hair." As the Greeks mapped the heavens, however, they discovered that comets were not stars at all. So they dropped *aster* from the name, leaving only *kometes,* which later became simply "comets."

Aristotle, around 350 B.C., pondered the meaning of comets. He knew that they do not travel in regular orbits like the stars and planets, therefore he concluded they are not in outer space but in the earth's atmosphere. Their bright light, he believed, was created by patches of air that caught on fire.

Aristotle's theory held for nearly two centuries. Then, in A.D. 1473, a German astronomer, Regiomontanus, observed a comet for several nights and traced its elongated orbit. Two astronomers, Girolamo Fracastoro and Peter Apian, put another puzzle piece in place in 1532, with their observation that the comet's tail always faced away from the sun. And, in 1577, Tycho Brahe, after collecting observations of a single comet from points in Denmark, Germany, and Bohemia, decided that the comet was about 1 million miles (1.6 million km) out in space—far beyond the earth's atmosphere.

From the sixteenth century to our present day, knowledge and understanding of comets has continued to grow. Over two thousand comets are now known, but estimates of the total number of comets in the solar system range from about 150,000 up to 5 million.

In the Beginning

The first modern theory on the origin, or source, of comets was put forth by the Dutch astronomer Jan Hendrick Oort in 1950. According to Oort, a giant cloud of comets surrounds the planets of the solar system. These are, of course, just the nuclei of the comets. The coma, tails, and hydrogen cloud do not develop until the comet is near the sun.

The comet nuclei are much too small to be seen through a telescope. The best guess is that there are over 100 million of them in the Oort cloud. The cloud probably stretches from about 30,000 to 100,000 AU. This is far beyond the farthest planet, Pluto, which is only 40 AU from the sun. Even so, the Oort cloud of comets is much closer than the nearest star, Alpha Centauri, which is 271,000 AU distant.

The huge comet cloud orbits around the sun like the planets. Each of the comets, it is thought, moves at a speed of about one to two inches (25 to 50 mm) per second. Their orbits, though, are always changing. Passing stars exert a gravitational pull on their orbits. From time to time, some of the comets are forced out of their pathways. They are sent flying in toward the sun. As they get closer to the sun, they become visible to us on earth.

Most astronomers accept the existence of the Oort cloud, but they do not all agree on the origin of the comets in the cloud. The most popular view is that they are made up of material that was left over from the formation of the planets, nearly five billion years ago.

The comets, then, are thought to contain some of the raw materials that were present at the creation of the solar system. This material has not been affected by radiation from the sun or by the pressure of being formed into a planet. It probably has hardly been changed at all for some five billion years. Comets are the building blocks of the planets *before* they become planets.

A few astronomers disagree. They hold that in the distant past there was a tenth planet somewhere between Mars and Jupiter. In a tremendous explosion, this planet blew up. Most of the pieces became the comet nuclei in the Oort cloud. The rest became asteroids, which are mostly found in a belt between Mars and Jupiter.

Joseph Louis Lagrange in the late eighteenth century was the first to state another theory. He said that the comets were ejected from Jupiter by means of some sort of powerful volcano. The Lagrange idea is not widely accepted. So far, there is no known source of energy great enough to eject a comet-sized body from Jupiter. In 1953, however, a Russian astronomer, S. I. Vsekhsviatskii, restated Lagrange's so-called ejection theory. The comets come, he said, not from Jupiter but from the moons of Jupiter, where it takes less energy for them to escape into space.

Most Famous Comet

Halley's Comet is the best known of all comets. It can readily be seen even without a telescope. Its nucleus has a maximum diameter of three miles (5 km), and its coma is about 250,000 miles (400,000 km) wide. The last time the gas tail was observed, it stretched 94 million miles (150 million km).

Edmund Halley (1656–1742), an English astronomer, first saw the comet he was to make famous in August 1682. He traced the arc of its orbit. Had the same comet been seen from earth before? A check of old records and accounts revealed sightings of over twenty comets from the past. The comets of 1456, 1532, and 1607, he discovered, had followed roughly the same path as the 1682 comet he had seen. Each sighting occurred about seventy-five or seventy-six years after the previous one.

This evidence helped Halley decide that the comet seen in 1682 was indeed the same as those seen previously. His calculations showed that its orbit, a long ellipse, stretched from about 0.6 AU at perihelion, its point nearest the sun, to 34 AU at its aphelion, its most distant point

Edmund Halley, the English astronomer, was the first to calculate the orbit and period of the comet that was named after him.

These photographs of Halley's comet were taken on May 12 and 15, 1910.

from the sun. The orbit reached from within the orbit of the earth to beyond the orbit of Neptune. The variation in the period between seventy-five and over seventy-six years, Halley explained, is the result of the gravitational pull of Jupiter and the other planets on the comet as it swings through the solar system.

Halley used his calculations to predict the return of the comet in 1758. Unfortunately Halley died in 1742. But on Christmas Day 1758, a German farmer, Johann Georg Palitzch, reported sighting the comet. It has returned twice since then, in 1835 and 1910. Its last appearance marked its twenty-ninth return since it was first reported in 239 B.C.

Scientists are anticipating the next arrival of Halley's comet in 1985 and 1986. It will surely be the most fully and carefully observed event in the history of comets.

Spotting Comets

Four conditions must be met before a comet can be seen. The comet must be large; it must be near the sun; it must also be near the earth; and it must be visible at night.

The unpredictable nature of comets makes it impractical for astronomers to set out to discover new ones. Most comets, therefore, are first seen by amateurs, people who search for comets just for the fun of it.

You can become a comet-spotter by learning to recognize these celestial bodies. Look for comets in the sky on dark, clear nights. Try to locate objects that look fuzzy or hairy as compared to the stars. Be especially alert for bodies with the long comet tails extending out. While stars, because of their great distances from earth seem fixed in

A comet looks fuzzy or hairy as compared to the stars.

space, comets appear to be moving among the stars.

Look for the magazine *Sky and Telescope* in your local library. A monthly section called "Comet Digest" will give you more general information on hunting comets. Also, it will provide specific data on the return of periodic comets. You will learn in what part of the sky to look for comets at each time of the year.

The International Astronomical Union (IAU) has a single central office to collect information on comet sightings. If you think you have spotted a comet, send a telegram to:

Central Bureau for Astronomical Telegrams
Smithsonian Astrophysical Observatory
Cambridge, Massachusetts 02138

In your telegram give the comet's position, direction of motion, and brightness. The telegram will also serve as a written record of your find. If you do not wish to send a telegram, you may telephone (617) 864-5758.

If you discover a comet, it is named after you. West's Comet, Kohoutek's Comet, and Whipple's Comet were named after their discoverers. Halley's Comet is an exception. It was named after Halley, not because he was first to spot it but because he learned that it had appeared in the past and would return in the future.

Comets are known not only by name but by the year of discovery. A letter placed after the year indicates the order in which the comets are sighted. Later, when the new comets' perihelions are calculated, the letters are changed to Roman numerals showing the order in which the comets reach perihelion.

(near right) Dr. Louis Kohoutek discovered this comet in 1973. It is known as Comet Kohoutek 1973 XII. (far right) Edward Emerson Barnard, shown here as a young man, was the best-known comet spotter.

Dr. Lubos Kohoutek, for example, discovered a comet in 1973. It was named Kohoutek 1973f, meaning that it was the sixth comet found that year. The following year it was given its final identification, Kohoutek 1973 XII, which tells that it is the twelfth comet to reach perihelion in 1973. Occasionally several people find the same new comet. In that case, up to three names may be used. The Tago-Sato-Kosaka is a well-known example of a three-name comet. When one person finds more than a single comet, an Arabic numeral may be used after that person's name, as in Comet Tempel 2.

The most outstanding amateur comet-finder was Edward Emerson Barnard (1857–1923). Although he was always interested in astronomy, Barnard worked for many years as a photographer. He earned very little, and when he got married in 1881, he found it hard to make ends meet. During the first year of his marriage he discovered a comet, but because he did not let anyone know it, he got no credit for his sighting.

Later that year, though, Barnard discovered Comet 1881 VI. This time he announced his sighting and received a prize of two hundred dollars. With the money he started to build a house. And he continued to spend many hours at his telescope, searching for new comets. Barnard was lucky enough to find several more comets over the next few years. "And thus it finally came about," Barnard said, "that this house was built entirely out of comets." Eventually, Barnard became a professional astronomer, and he won lasting fame as the discoverer of the fifth moon of Jupiter.

Comet watching on a grand scale is being planned for the mid-1980s. NASA is designing an unmanned spacecraft that will take a close-up look at Halley's Comet during its next pass by earth in 1985 and 1986.

The spacecraft will be equipped with cameras, spectroscopes, and other scientific instruments to record and measure a number of different aspects of the comet. A smaller probe craft will separate from the large one and fly through the coma of the comet, collecting particles and gases and measuring the magnetism. A radio on board will send the results back to earth.

After finishing its work on Halley's Comet, the NASA spacecraft will head out to the space beyond Mars. Its destination is a rendezvous with Comet Tempel 2. While following this comet to its perihelion, it will observe the changes that take place as the comet approaches the sun. Finally, the spacecraft will crash into the nucleus of Tempel 2. The exact conditions of the crash, it is hoped, will tell scientists more about the structure and materials of the nucleus. Altogether, the spacecraft will spend about four years in space and cover some 1.6 billion miles (2.5 billion km).

It is hoped that this exciting mission will fill in missing bits of information on both Halley's Comet and Tempel 2, and give us a more complete understanding of all comets.

(left) Astronomers have already plotted the orbit of Halley's comet when it will be near earth in 1985 and 1986. (below) This is a drawing of the spacecraft being designed to study Halley's comet and Comet Tempel 2 in the mid-1980s.

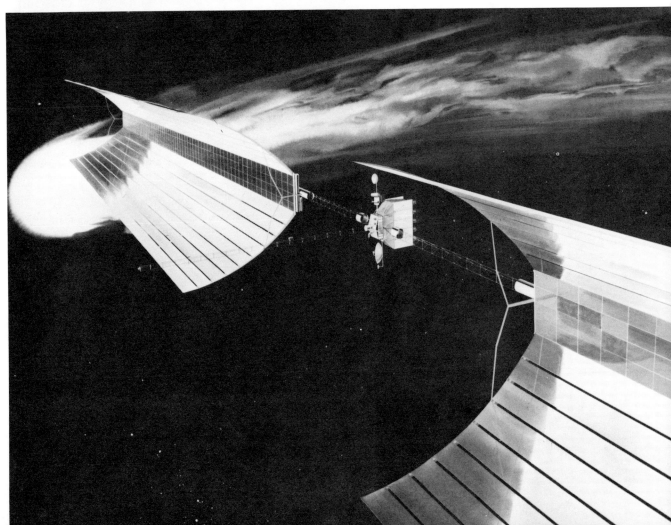

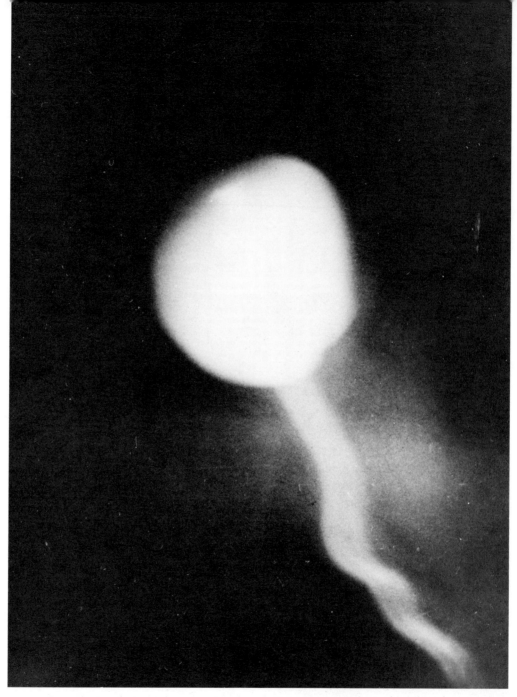

When a meteor produces enough light to cast shadows it is called a fireball. This rare photograph of a fireball was taken by Charles M. Brown in New Mexico on March 24, 1933.

3 / Meteors

Coming to Terms with Meteors

You may call the flash of light you see streaking across the sky on a clear dark night a shooting star or a falling star. To astronomers, though, they are meteors. By definition, a meteor is a tiny particle from outer space that produces light as it enters the earth's atmosphere.

When a very large meteor enters the atmosphere, it may produce a great deal of light. If it appears brighter in the sky than a bright planet, it is more proper to call the object a fireball. Some say that the particle is a fireball if it gives off enough light to cast shadows on earth. When a fireball explodes in the atmosphere it is called a bolide.

The solid object in space, before it enters the earth's atmosphere and becomes a meteor, is a meteoroid. Technically, a meteoroid is an object, smaller than an asteroid and larger than a molecule, that is found within the space of the solar system.

Only a tiny percentage of all the meteoroids in space enter the earth's atmosphere to become meteors or fireballs. Of those that do,

(left) This is a stony meteorite. It is similar in appearance to an ordinary earth rock. (right) Some meteorites are mostly metal, usually a mixture of iron and nickel.

only a small number survive the flight through the atmosphere to land on earth. Those that do fall to earth are known as meteorites.

Some meteorites that have landed on earth have shown astronomers that meteoroids can have a mass of many tons. Most meteoroids, though, are very small and light. They do not weigh more than a speck of dust or a grain of sand.

Meteoroids vary according to the material of which they are made. The most common are probably the stony meteoroids. Almost completely mineral, they have just tiny traces of metal. They look like earth rocks.

Other meteoroids are made mostly of metal. These meteoroids are often called irons because they are about 90 percent iron. Nickel makes up most of the remaining 10 percent.

A third type of meteoroids are the stony-irons. These are a mixture of rocklike minerals and metals.

Astronomers now believe that meteoroids move through space at speeds between 18 and 41 miles (30 and 65 km) per second. Inside the earth's atmosphere the meteor's speed is only about 7.5 miles (12 km) per second. This might not sound very fast to you. But remember that the earth moves through space at 18.5 miles (30 km) per second. In a head-on collision, the meteorite strikes the earth at a speed of 7.5 + 18.5 (12 + 30 km) or 26 miles (42 km) per second, which works out to 1,560 miles (2,250 km) an hour. This is more than thirty times as fast as the speediest rifle bullet!

A meteoroid is invisible until it enters the earth's atmosphere and becomes a meteor. What makes it visible? The light actually comes from the atoms in the air of the atmosphere through which the meteor passes. The meteor strips the electrons from the atoms in the air, and as these atoms regain the missing electrons, they emit tiny bursts of light. It is the trail of these light-emitting atoms that we see in the night sky and call a meteor.

Meteors Through History

In the Bible Joshua says, "The Lord cast down great stones from heaven." The ancient Greeks describe "a stone the size of a chariot" that fell from the sky around the year 476 B.C. Plutarch, Livy and Pliny were Roman scholars who wrote accounts of meteors and meteorites.

From the dawn of history, meteors and meteorites were believed to have special meaning. Were they perhaps stars that had fallen from the heavens? Messengers from God? The Chinese buried any meteorites they found in the hope that they would ensure a good harvest. Meteorites were objects of worship in the Roman temples of Diana in Ephesus and Venus in Cyprus.

When a star-shaped meteorite fell around the year 700 B.C., it was widely thought that whoever owned the meteorite would rule the world. The Roman emperor Numa Pomplius gained possession of the meteorite. He then had eleven copies made to fool any thieves who might try to steal it from him.

The Mogul emperor Jahangir had another way to use a meteorite to conquer the world. He ordered that an iron meteorite that fell in 1621 be made into a sword. With the sword he was certain he would never be defeated in battle.

The oldest known meteorite still in existence fell on the German village of Ensisheim on November 16, 1492. To Emperor Maximilian, the meteorite was a sign of God's anger with the Turks. This relic from

(left) A meteoroid is invisible until it enters the earth's atmosphere and becomes a meteor, as shown in this photograph. (above) This print from the time shows the fall of a meteorite in the German village of Ensisheim in 1492.

space can still be seen in the Ensisheim town hall. It is a stony meteorite, weighing about 280 pounds (127 kg).

Meteors and meteorites were not considered worthy of serious study until near the end of the eighteenth century. In 1798, two German students, Brandes and Benzenberg, observed the same meteor from two points several miles apart. Later, when they compared notes, they realized that meteors are not nearly as far out in space as the planets or stars; nor are they as close as bolts of lightning, which were believed by some to cause meteors.

Then, on April 26, 1803, some reliable witnesses saw a meteorite land in the French town of L'Aigle. A number of astronomers set out to investigate the incident. Their examination launched a new science, the science of meteorites, or meteoritics. Astronomers and other scientists have since learned a good deal about what meteors are, where they come from, and how they behave.

The Findings

There are certain times of the year when many more meteors are visible than at other times. Since the mid-nineteenth century, these dates have been associated with certain comets.

Each time the earth crosses the orbit of one of these comets, there are suddenly many more meteors to be seen. A German astronomer, E. Weiss, predicted that the earth would pass through the orbit of Biela's Comet on November 28, 1872. He foretold that there would be a big display on that day. While his forecast was off by twenty-four hours, the especially large number of meteors did appear on the twenty-seventh day of November 1872.

This association between meteors and comets seemed to point to a simple explanation for the origin of meteors. Meteors are nothing more than dust particles that escape from the comets as they speed in their orbits near the sun. The tiny particles are the remains of disintegrating comets.

This theory did not work too well. One difficulty was that it did not explain the origin of all meteors. A certain number of meteors are obviously much larger than any of the particles found in comets. Also, only some twelve dates of increased meteor activity could be associated with comets. Where do the larger meteors come from? What is the source of all the other meteors?

The debris of comets is no longer thought to be the only source of meteoroids. Meteoroids may arise from collisions between asteroids. When two asteroids collide, the great force probably breaks off hunks of material. Then when the planets and stars line up in a particular way, their gravity sends some of these fragments into the earth's atmosphere. From earth, they are seen as meteors.

Evidence for this theory on the source of meteoroids comes from their close connection with asteroids. Asteroids, it is believed, have a chemical makeup similar to that of earth. They contain rock on the outside, or crust, with a central core of metal. This fits in perfectly with our knowledge of the three types of meteoroids: stony (from the crust of the asteroid), iron (from the core of the asteroid), and stony-iron (from between the crust and the core).

Further evidence for the asteroid origin of meteoroids came in April 1959. Two separate observatories in Czechoslovakia, by a bit of good luck, photographed the fall of the same stony meteorite on the Czech city of Pribram. By comparing the two photos, the astronomers were able to calculate the path of the meteor. The results showed that it originated in the belt of asteroids between Mars and Jupiter.

Most astronomers now accept both theories on the sources of meteoroids. Meteoroids originate from dust of comets *and* from fragments resulting from asteroid collisions. They say that the tiny meteoroids come from the comets. The larger ones come from the asteroids.

Meteoroids and Life

A meteorite fell in Murchison, Australia, on September 28, 1969. A sample was sent to the scientists at NASA's Ames Research Center in California. They studied the meteorite to see if it carried any evidence of life in space.

The scientists found traces of eighteen amino acids in the stone. Amino acids are the building blocks of life, from which the all-important protein molecules are formed. But scientists were unable to answer the crucial question: Where did the amino acids on the meteoroid come from? Were they present on the meteoroid in space? Or

The meteorite that fell on Murchison, Australia in 1969 was found to contain traces of amino acids.

METRIC 1 2 3 4 5

were they picked up on the stone's trip through the atmosphere or its landing on the ground? One researcher pointed out that a single fingerprint could deposit a number of amino acids on the meteorite.

To learn more, they compared their results with studies done on a meteorite that fell in Murray, Kentucky, in 1950. The earlier meteorite also contained eighteen amino acids.

A most important finding in 1978 cast further light on the subject. A number of meteorites were found frozen in the antarctic ice. They had fallen far from most sources of contamination. Like moon rocks, they were kept as sterile as possible. Close examination showed the presence on these meteoroids, too, of several amino acids.

Many scientists now believe that the amino acids, the first step toward living plants and animals, are present in space. Life on earth may have been triggered by the arrival of these amino acids—perhaps on a meteorite. Continued studies on a new group of meteorites found in Antarctica in March 1980 are probing deeper into the possible connection between meteors and the origin of life on earth.

Meteor Falls and Finds

Look up into the sky on the next clear, dark night. You should see an average of about six meteors an hour. Most will be visible for just a few seconds before they burn themselves out. If you see a typical meteor, its light will appear when it is between 81 and 59 miles (130 and 95 km) above earth. By the time it is down to a height of 50 miles (80 km) it usually disintegrates and disappears.

On a few nights of the year the average number of meteors you see will jump from six up to as many as fifty or more an hour. This great

increase in meteor activity is called a meteor shower.

The most spectacular meteor shower occurred on the night of November 13, 1833. Observers reported seeing meteors "as thick as snowflakes during a snow storm." Watchers in the southeastern part of the United States estimated that anywhere from 100,000 to 300,000 meteors appeared during one hour. The shower took place just as earth was crossing through the orbit of Comet Tempel 1866 I. The comet vanished from view long ago, but the debris it left in the sky furnishes the meteors for the shower that is seen in the middle of November every year.

The meteors during a shower fall in parallel paths, but an optical illusion makes it seem that they are coming from one point in the sky. This point is referred to as the radiant. Meteor showers take their name from the constellation in the apparent direction of the radiant. Since the radiant for the mid-November shower appears in the direction of the constellation Leo, it is known as the Leonid shower.

The biggest annual meteor shower comes on August eleventh. The radiant appears to be in the constellation Perseus, so it is called the Perseid shower. It is caused by the earth's passage through the orbit of Comet 1862 III. You may want to look for such other well-known showers as the Eta Aquarids on May fourth (associated with Halley's Comet), Draconids on October tenth, Orionids on October twentieth, Taurids on November first, and Ursids on December twenty-second.

Many of the streaks of light seen during a shower are believed to be caused by micrometeors, which are tiny microscopic specks of matter. The dustlike particles are the result of comet disintegration. Large-sized meteorites rarely, if ever, fall to earth during a shower.

49

The most spectacular meteor shower of all time was supposed to have occurred on November 13, 1833. The meteors were "as thick as snowflakes," as the artist shows in this old drawing.

This photo was taken on November 17, 1966, of the Leonid meteor shower.

On a typical day, though, about one thousand tons of micrometeorites land on the earth. They fall as a fine dust that we do not even notice. Some 500 billion tons (454 billion metric tons) of micrometeorites have already fallen throughout the history of the earth. Every time you walk through a field you are stepping on micrometeorites. Every time you sweep a floor you are cleaning some away.

Only a small number of meteorites are large enough to be seen and recovered. Somewhere between two hundred and two thousand of these larger meteorites strike the earth each year. More than 70 percent of the earth's surface is covered with water. Therefore, most of these meteorites fall into the water and are lost forever. Only about four or five meteorites a year are actually found and collected.

If you are *very* lucky, you may see a large meteoroid, say as big as a basketball, enter the earth's atmosphere. This big meteoroid produces a fireball. For a few seconds it lights up an area as large as several states. The fireball sometimes explodes in a tremendous flash, or a bolide, before it strikes the earth. Other times it lands on earth as a meteorite.

Your chances of seeing a meteorite land on the earth are slim. The observed landing of a meteorite is called a fall. Most of the meteorites recovered from falls are stone. A meteorite that is not seen falling, but is found later, is called a find. Most finds are iron.

Can you guess why most meteorites recovered from falls are stone, and most recovered from finds are iron?

Stony meteorites look very much like earth rocks. They are hard to recognize. Unless you see one coming down in a fall, it is not likely that you will spot it among the earth rocks. It is especially hard to locate stony meteorites in rocky areas. That is why many more stony meteorites are found in the farmland of the Midwest than in the rocky fields of New England. Iron meteorites are easy to pick out among earth rocks. Therefore, many are recovered from finds.

Meteors create great heat as they fall through the atmosphere. The

Meteorites are often covered with a thin, dark coat called a fusion crust.

METRIC 1 2 3 4 5 6

heat melts the outer layers of the meteor, forming a thin coat, called a fusion crust. It is often as smooth as glass and either black or dark brown in color.

Meteorites that strike the earth, though, are either cold or warm, seldom hot. In January 1869 a meteorite landed on a frozen lake in Sweden. It did not even melt the ice. A meteorite that was recovered minutes after landing in Wisconsin, in July 1917, was covered with frost. No meteorite anywhere, has ever burned or scorched the plant life where it landed.

Meteorites are not hot when they land because they come from very cold regions of outer space. Passage through the atmosphere heats the outside layers of meteors, forming the fusion crust. But chips of the crust flake off, preventing the heat from reaching the inside of the meteorite.

This flaking also leaves the meteorites with their characteristic pitted look. They look like irregular balls of clay indented with giant thumbprints.

Meteors That Have Made History
The largest meteorite found on earth is the so-called Hoba iron that

landed near Grootfontein, southwest Africa. This huge find measures about 10 feet by 10 feet (3 m by 3 m) across the top, and is about 3 feet (1 m) thick. The Hoba iron has been left half buried in the ground where it landed. Could that be because it weighs about 60 tons (54 metric tons)?

Iron is less likely to break apart than stone. That is why more large iron meteorites have been found than stones. The heaviest stone meteorite was part of a fall in Kirin, China, on March 8, 1976. Fragments of stone meteorites came down over an area of some 195 square miles (500 square km). The biggest single piece has a mass of 3,894 pounds (1770 kg).

Meteorites have been striking the earth since the beginning of recorded history. Yet, no city or town has ever been destroyed. No person has ever been killed by a meteorite. The closest near accident that we know of occurred on November 30, 1954, in Sylacauga, Alabama. Mrs. E. H. Hodges was resting after lunch on the couch in her living room. Suddenly an 8.5 pound (3.85 kg) meteorite tore through the roof of her house. The stone hit and bounced off the radio, striking Mrs. Hodges in the leg. It caused only a minor bruise.

Surely, over the billions of years of the earth's history many giant meteorites have landed on our planet. But weathering, erosion, and plant growth have erased most of their traces. One clear sign of a meteorite fall that you can still see today is the Meteor Crater in the desert near Winslow, Arizona.

The Meteor Crater is a gigantic hole in the ground. It is nearly in the form of a circle, with a diameter of 4,265 feet (1,300 m). The depth is about 509 feet (155 m). The meteorite itself is not in the crater. Fragments, though, are scattered all around the site. Within a 4 mile radius (6.5 km) about 30 tons (27 metric tons) of small meteoric metal bits have been collected.

Studies show that the crater was formed about 24,000 years ago. It was most likely made by a huge iron meteorite, with a mass of perhaps 100,000 tons (90,000 metric tons), and a diameter of 82 feet (25 m). The meteorite slammed into the ground at a speed of 6 miles (10 km) per second. On impact it exploded with the force of 30 million tons of TNT going off all at once. The powerful explosion shattered the meteorite completely. Most of it vaporized and changed into gas. The rest was scattered as small metal fragments around the rim of the crater.

Firsthand accounts and direct evidence tell us about an immense fireball that appeared early on the morning of June 30, 1908, over the remote Tunguska region of Siberia. People up to 38 miles (60 km) away

The Meteor Crater in the desert near Winslow, Arizona, was probably formed by a gigantic iron meteorite about 24,000 years ago. The crater is nearly a mile across.

felt the clothes on their bodies grow very hot. Windows broke as far away as 50 miles (80 km). A passing train, 440 miles (700 km) distant, was almost knocked off its tracks. The shock waves were felt all over Europe and throughout the rest of the world.

Scientists entering the area found that trees had been completely flattened in a circle with a diameter of over 100 miles (180 km). Assuming that all the destruction had been caused by a meteorite, they sought a central crater. But there was no crater to be found.

For years, many fanciful explanations were offered for the Tunguska incident: A nuclear-powered alien spacecraft had exploded while trying to land. A black hole from outer space had come to earth.

None answered the basic questions: What caused all the destruction? If the cause was an object, why was there neither a crater nor any trace of the object?

A group of Russian scientists announced in January 1980, after six years of study, that it was indeed a meteorite that had landed in Siberia. The object had been made of stone, with a mass of at least 4,000 tons (3,600 metric tons). Because it was stone and so large, it was unable to withstand the powerful forces created by its fiery plunge through the atmosphere. Therefore, it became a bolide, exploding before impact. The heat and shock waves from the explosion caused all the damage over the vast area of land.

One of the key clues that helped to solve the mystery was the discovery of several tiny diamondlike stones at the site. These stones are formed only as the result of tremendous pressure. The two known sources of such intense pressure are found inside the earth, or as the result of two solid bodies, such as meteoroids or asteroids, colliding

The trees over hundreds of miles in the Tunguska region of Siberia were destroyed when a giant bolide exploded in the air on June 30, 1908.

in space. Since the stones had obviously not risen to the earth's surface, they must have been brought to earth by a meteorite that had disintegrated in the explosion.

The meteorites that fell in Arizona and Siberia caused great local damage. But, early in 1980, some scientists learned more about a meteorite that fell 65 million years ago. This meteorite did more than impact the face of the earth. It changed the life on earth for all time.

Fossils found by a scientist Luis Alvarez and his coworkers showed that 65 million years ago about half the plant and animal species on earth, including dinosaurs, became extinct. Alvarez's theory is that a giant meteorite hit the earth at that time. This meteorite was about 6 miles (10 km) in diameter, and struck with the force of 100 million tons of TNT. The explosion raised a tremendous cloud of dust.

For the following three to five years the dust hung over the earth. It blocked the sunlight, and without sunlight, large numbers of plants died, as did the animals that ate the plants. Many of the plant and animal species disappeared during those few years.

Alvarez based his theory on studies of some limestone deposits in Italy and Denmark. At the level he estimated to be about 65 million years old, he found a layer containing extra amounts of the element iridium. Iridium does not normally appear on the surface of the earth. It is found either in the earth's core, or in outer space. A likely source for the iridium, therefore, may have been the dust from the remains of the large meteorite that came to earth long, long ago.

More proof is needed. One line of research expects to find traces of the crater or other evidence of a fallen meteorite. Another hopes to find a different layer of iridium-rich rock that can be associated with another major upheaval of life on earth.

Meteors in Your Life

The best time to look for meteors is on a dark, clear night after midnight. More meteors are seen then because after midnight, you are on the front part of the globe. This section is advancing through space as the earth orbits around the sun. You are more likely to run into meteors while you are on the front side of the earth than before midnight when you are on the back side.

Just think of driving an automobile through a rain shower. Do more raindrops fall on the front windshield of the auto or the back window? Unless the wind is blowing strongly from behind, more rain strikes the front windshield because the front of the car is pushing against the drops. Meteors are like raindrops in that they are more likely to bump into the side of the earth that is moving forward.

If you see a meteor, jot down as much information about it as you can: At what time did you see the meteor? How long did the light last? What color was it? In what direction was it traveling?

Should you see a meteorite fall, or come upon a meteorite find, answer the questions a meteoriticist might ask: Exactly when and where did it fall? When did you get to the scene? Did it feel warm or cold to the touch? What was its size and weight? Did it create a crater? How large? What kind of soil did it land in?

As soon as you sight a meteor or find a meteorite, write or call one of the organizations that collects such information. Two of the major ones are:

The American Museum of Natural History
Central Park West and 79th Street
New York, N.Y. 10024
(212) 873-1300

Smithsonian Institution
14th Street and Constitution Avenue, N.W.
Washington, D.C. 20560
(202) 357-1300

4 / Asteroids

Mountains in Space

Between the planets Mars and Jupiter there is a swarm of flying objects that are commonly known as asteroids. They have been described as "mountains in space." The International Astronomical Union uses the name minor planets, but many astronomers still call them asteroids. These same bodies are also called planetoids because they resemble planets.

Most asteroids are found in a belt at a distance of 2.1 to 3.5 AU from the sun. The asteroid belt is located between Mars, at an average orbit distance of 1.5 AU, and Jupiter, which is at 5.2 AU.

As many as 400,000 asteroids with diameters larger than six-tenths of a mile (1 km) may occupy the asteroid belt. Of these, only 2,000 or so have been seen and identified. The largest, Ceres, has a diameter of 638 miles (1,020 km). Only 20 asteroids, approximately, have diameters over 100 miles (160 km). The smallest asteroid on record was discovered in October 1976. It has a diameter of 656 feet (200 m). Asteroids range down in size to those that are much too small to be seen with a telescope.

Asteroids vary in shape almost as much as they do in size. Some asteroids are spherical, about the same shape as the planet earth. Others, though, are irregular, with rough, uneven surfaces. Eros, to take one example, looks like a long, skinny, deeply pitted football. It is about 23 miles (36 km) long, and 9 miles (14 km) wide across the middle.

The orbits of the asteroids are mostly ellipses, with periods between two and six years. Astronomers estimate that if all the asteroids were combined into a single body, this body would have a total mass equal to about 1/1,600th that of the earth. To put it another way, all the asteroids together weigh less than 1/20th the weight of the moon.

Diagram showing the asteroid belt.

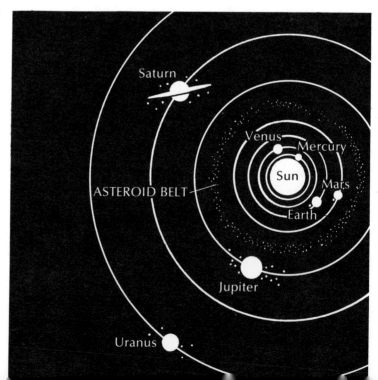

Astronomers gather most information on asteroids indirectly. To determine their size, they measure the amount of sunlight reflected by the surface of the asteroid. The bigger the surface, the more light is reflected. More exact measurements can be made by observing an asteroid as it passes in front of a star. The time it takes to pass by is a measure of its size. This method is called occultation. It was used in 1978 to determine that the diameter of Pallas was exactly 336.25 miles (538 km).

Measurements of reflected light reveal the irregular shapes of some asteroids. As these bodies move in their orbits they topple end over end. This varies the amount of reflected light. Changes in the light indicate surfaces of different sizes and shapes.

The light reflected from an asteroid can be passed through a spectroscope. This shows the chemical makeup of the object. In general, asteroids are made up of much the same minerals and metals as are the basic rocks of the earth and the other earthlike planets.

Starlike Bodies

On January 1, 1801, the first day of the nineteenth century, the Italian monk and astronomer Giuseppe Piazzi was studying the skies through his telescope. He was preparing a catalogue of star positions. On the next night, he noticed that one of the stars, a point of light he had seen the previous evening, had moved. A further check on the third night showed Piazzi that the same star had strayed even farther from its original position.

Stars appear to remain in one spot. So the moving object could not be a star. The planets, being much closer than the stars, look like round discs through a telescope. This object did not look like a round disc so it could not be a planet. For a while Piazzi thought that it might be a comet. But comets appear fuzzy through a telescope. This object appeared to be a clean point of light, most like a star.

For six weeks Piazzi followed the mysterious object as it moved slowly across the sky. Then he fell sick, and missed several days at his telescope. When he recovered and went back to work, he could no longer find the object in the sky.

Piazzi sent copies of his findings to other astronomers. Perhaps one of them might locate the elusive object he had found and then lost. But no one had seen it or knew where to find it.

The German astronomer and mathematician Karl Friedrich Gauss heard about Piazzi's object. At the time, Gauss was working out a new way to calculate the orbits of objects in space. Using the figures Piazzi supplied, he put his method to the test.

Gauss's results showed that the body was really a small planetlike object in an orbit between Mars and Jupiter. He calculated its orbit, and in October predicted where it would appear in the sky over the following months. Based on the Gauss prediction, Baron von Zach, a German astronomer, found Piazzi's object again on December 7, 1801.

A few weeks later Heinrich Olbers, also using Gauss's figures, saw the same object. It was given the name Ceres Ferdinandea. Later the name was shortened to Ceres. Since it looked something like a star through the telescope, the British astronomer Sir William Herschel coined the name asteroid, meaning starlike body.

After the discovery of the first asteroid, a few others were located in short order. Pallas was discovered in 1802, Juno in 1804, and Vesta

This photograph was taken with a three-hour exposure. It shows how stars appear to remain in one spot, while an asteroid creates a trail of light.

in 1807. Then a stretch of nearly forty years followed with no asteroid finds. This was quite a contrast to the second half of the nineteenth century, though, when more than three hundred new asteroids were sighted.

Up until the last decade of the nineteenth century, all sightings were made by peering at the skies through a telescope. Around 1891, astronomers began to use telescopes with cameras attached, which increased the rate of asteroid discoveries. Today about two thousand asteroids are known, and the number is increasing annually.

At first, asteroids were named after mythological beings. As well-known names were used up, other names began to be used. Now when a new asteroid is found, it is identified by the year of discovery and two letters. The first letter indicates the date of discovery by half months. Thus A is the first half of January, B is the second half, C is the first half of February, and so on.

The second letter indicates the order of discovery within that half month. Once the finding is checked by other astronomers, it is given a temporary number. For example, 1976AA is an asteroid that was found in the first half of January 1976, and it was the first one found during that period. Later it was given the number 2060 and named Aten. The number refers to the order of discovery of all asteroids. The name was chosen by the person who found it.

Where Asteroids Come From

For the longest time, asteroids were thought to come from the explosion of a planet that had been in orbit between Mars and Jupiter. According to an astronomical formula based on the distances between the planets, there should be a planet in that space.

Today this theory is no longer widely accepted. The total mass of all asteroids is much less than even the smallest planet. If asteroids had once been a planet, what happened to the remaining mass? Also, there is no known source for the tremendous amount of energy that would be necessary for a planet to explode.

Asteroids are now believed to be material that is left over from the time when the planets were first being formed. The explanation goes like this: The two largest bodies of the solar system are the sun and Jupiter. They produce the strongest gravity. The sun is larger and has the greater gravitational pull. The objects in the asteroid belt, however, are much closer to Jupiter. Jupiter's gravitational pull on these bodies, therefore, just about balances the gravitational pull of the sun. The nearly equal pull in two opposite directions on these objects prevents them from coming together to form a planet.

The fact that many asteroids have irregular shapes is explained another way: Many thousands of asteroids orbit in a narrow belt in space. Collisions and smash-ups are bound to occur. When two asteroids collide with enough speed and force, hunks and chips are knocked off both of them. Thus asteroids take on irregular forms and rough surfaces.

Strange Asteroids

Hektor is one of the oddest of all asteroids. Its fascinating behavior and appearance are now being carefully studied by astronomers William K. Hartmann and Dale Cruikshank.

Hektor varies greatly in brightness. At times this asteroid is more than three times as bright as at other times. Usually this variance means that the asteroid is three times as long as it is wide. But Hartmann and Cruikshank have a different theory. They think that Hektor might be formed of two asteroids that collided at slow speeds—and stuck together.

According to their figures, if two small asteroids, less than 80 miles

(126 km) in diameter, bump while traveling at a speed no greater than a few hundred miles per hour, they might just stick together like two balls of clay. Asteroids that are bigger in size or faster in speed, because of their greater momentum, might be expected to shatter and rip each other apart.

If the Hartmann and Cruikshank theory is right, then Hektor looks like two immense basketballs glued together. The scientists are now attempting a spectroscopic analysis of the two opposite ends of Hektor. Should this analysis detect any difference in chemical composition it will confirm their model of its shape.

Hektor is a strange asteroid. Astronomers think it looks like two basketballs stuck together.

On June 7, 1978, asteroid Herculina occulted a star. A group of astronomers were carefully observing the event. They were trying to get an accurate measurement of Herculina's size. They found it to be 150 miles (241 km) in diameter. To their amazement, though, the star's light blinked out again—after Herculina passed!

Some quick calculations showed that there was another body, about 620 miles (998 km) from Herculina. It has a diameter of 28 miles (45 km). Could this be a moon in orbit around Herculina?

In December of the same year, a similar finding was made with asteroid Melpomene. On the basis of these reports, some astronomers are beginning to think that some asteroids may have natural satellites circling about them.

Astronomers have long known about Phobos and Deimos, the two moons, or satellites, circling the planet Mars. Now, though, they are looking at these two bodies with new interest. It is thought likely that the two moons are actually asteroids. Somehow they were captured by the gravity of Mars, and have remained in orbit around the planet. In 1976 NASA's Viking spacecraft landed on Mars. It sent close-up photographs of the moons back to earth by radio. The photographs show that the moons have irregular shapes. This, along with their small size, helps to confirm the idea that they are really asteroids.

Asteroids Out of Place

Ninety-five percent of all asteroids are found in the asteroid belt between Mars and Jupiter. There are, however, some surprising exceptions.

The Trojans are a group of perhaps a thousand asteroids that travel

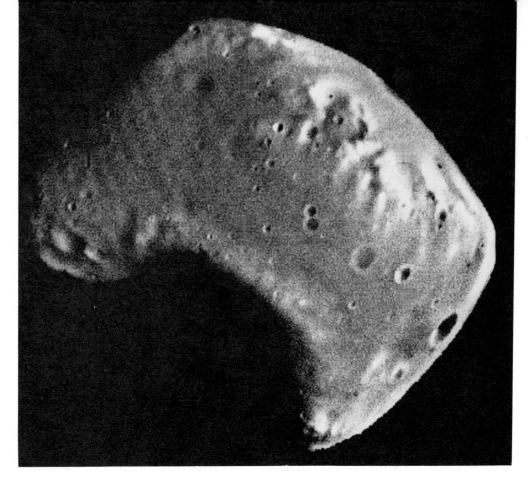

Deimos, one of the two moons of Mars, is shown in this close-up photograph taken in 1976 by the Viking spacecraft. Many astronomers now believe that both moons are asteroids that were captured by Mars' gravity.

in Jupiter's orbit, some ahead of the planet, some behind. The combined gravitational pulls of Jupiter and the sun hold them in place. The Trojans, unlike the other asteroids, are dark red in color.

A most important asteroid discovery was recently announced. Charles Kowal, an astronomer working at the Hale Observatory in California, was photographing the night sky in October 1977. He was carefully examining the photographs under a microscope, when he noticed a faint trail of light. He asked other astronomers to photograph the same area of sky. They, too, saw the mysterious trail.

Drawing on various observations, Kowal calculated the source at a distance of about 16 AU. That placed it between the orbits of Saturn and Uranus. But it was a much smaller body than either of these two giant planets. Kowal's object, he guessed, had a diameter between 100 and 400 miles (160 and 640 km).

What was this object? It was much too small to be a planet. And it was much too large, by a figure of about a hundred times, to be a comet. Nor did it look or behave like one. Finally, it could not be an asteroid since no asteroid had ever been found beyond the orbit of Saturn.

The more he thought about it, the more Kowal became convinced that the object was, in fact, an asteroid. Perhaps it had been orbiting in the asteroid belt with all of the other asteroids in the past. Then, because of a collision or some other force, it had been knocked out of its orbit and sent into the distant one.

Kowal named the asteroid Chiron. It remains the farthest asteroid known. Other astronomers, though, are now searching the skies for other asteroids at this distance, far beyond where they are usually found.

In recent years some asteroids have come very near to the orbit of our planet earth. The closest recorded encounter took place in October 1937. The asteroid Hermes came within about 500,000 miles (800,000 km). Hermes has a diameter of under 2.4 miles (1.5 km). It is quite small as compared to the other known asteroids. Yet, if Hermes had struck earth, scientists estimate it would have exploded with the force of 20,000 one-megaton hydrogen bombs. The explosions would have been powerful enough to destroy a country the size of Switzerland.

The statistical chance of such a collision between earth and an asteroid is very slight. One estimate puts it at about one in thirty thousand. Considering the number of asteroids that pass close to earth, such an event could take place no more than once every hundred thousand years!

A few other asteroids have passed near the earth over the last fifty years. Adonis approached in February 1936, 900,000 miles (1.5 million km); Apollo in April 1932, 1.9 million miles (3 million km); Icarus in June 1968, 4 million miles (6.4 million km); and Eros in January 1975, 14 million miles (22.5 million km).

These asteroids are part of a special group called Apollo-Amor objects. The first Apollo-Amor object was identified in 1932. Since then astronomers have discovered nearly thirty more. They are named after the gods of Greek mythology.

Apollo-Amor objects are small asteroids, ranging in diameter from about one-eighth of a mile (0.2 km) to a maximum of 5 miles (8 km). They have an average diameter of some 1.4 miles (2.2 km). Most important of all, these asteroids have orbits that take them inside the orbit of the earth. All have perihelions of less than 1 AU.

Research into the nature of the Apollo-Amor bodies is bringing together comets, meteors and asteroids—the three types of nonplanet bodies in the solar system. Scientists now think that the Apollo-Amor objects are the main producers of craters larger than 3 miles (5 km) on earth, as well as on Mercury, Venus and the moon. What we have long called meteors and meteorites may really be Apollo-Amor objects, or asteroids.

There is also the possibility that Apollo-Amor objects may be degassed or extinct comets. As comets orbit near the sun, radiation from the star drives out the ices in the nucleus. The ices turn into gas and release particles of dust. But what happens to the rest of the particles in the nucleus, after all the gas is gone? Could "dead" comets become Apollo-Amor objects? The search is on to find answers to these questions.

The odds of an Apollo-Amor object striking the earth over the next hundreds or thousands of years are very slim. Yet, scientists are devoting some thought to the possibility. One group of experts at the Massachusetts Institute of Technology (MIT) is looking at this problem: Suppose we find an Apollo-Amor object following a collision course with the earth. What should we do?

The hope is to prevent such an encounter. These scientists propose that we first collect a large number of rockets, able to be sent into space, high above the earth's atmosphere. Then, we should equip these rockets with the most powerful hydrogen bombs that are available. And we should set them to explode when they hit the asteroid. Then, the small fragments of the shattered Apollo-Amor object would either burn up in the atmosphere, or would fall harmlessly to earth.

Other scientists at MIT are asking: How can we use the Apollo-Amor bodies for the good of humanity?

These scientists are exploring two new ideas. Why not attach what they call "mass drivers" to the objects? Mass drivers are engines that run on fuel found on the asteroids themselves. Then, use the objects as ready-made space stations. Ride them through the skies to accomplish the missions now being planned for earth-built space stations.

Or, why not land people on the Apollo-Amor objects and establish colonies? The metals and minerals that they likely contain could be used to build the spacecraft and space stations needed for further space exploration. Even though only 30 Apollo-Amor bodies have been recorded, there are between 750 and 1,000 of these objects in space. Might they prove to be a source of raw materials not easily obtainable on earth?

This is a very exciting time in the history of comets, meteors and asteroids. We are finding more and more surprises in the "debris in the sky." New discoveries are giving us vital clues to the origin of the planets and the early history of our solar system. And they are helping us to unlock mysteries that range from the origin of life on earth to the presence of other, unknown objects in the far reaches of space.

Glossary

Amino Acids Molecules that serve as the building blocks of proteins.

Aphelion The point in an orbit farthest from the sun.

Apollo-Amor Objects A group of small-sized asteroids whose orbits bring them near earth.

Asteroid A small, solid planet-like body that moves in an orbit around the sun.

Asteroid Belt A band of space between Mars and Jupiter where most of the asteroids are located.

Astronomical Unit The distance between the earth and the sun, equal to 93 million miles (150 million km). Abbreviated as AU.

Astronomy The science that studies the materials and forces in the universe beyond the earth's atmosphere.

Atom The smallest unit of an element.

Bolide A very bright meteor or fireball that explodes in space.

Coma (of a comet) The envelope of gas and dust that surrounds the solid nucleus of a comet.

Comet A small body of ice and dust in orbit around the sun, consisting of a nucleus, coma, hydrogen cloud, and one or two tails.

Electron A subatomic particle of negative charge that normally moves around the nucleus of an atom.

Ellipse A geometric curve that varies from a flattened circle to a cigar shape.

Fall The observed landing of a meteorite on earth.

Falling Star Another word for meteor.

Find A meteorite that was not seen falling, but found on earth.

Fireball A meteor that produces enough light to cast shadows on earth.

Fusion Crust The thin, smooth, dark crust of meteors; caused by the heat generated by the passage through the earth's atmosphere.

Head (of a comet) The central nucleus and surrounding coma of the comet, not including the tail.

Hydrogen Cloud Large clouds of hydrogen gas that were recently found to surround the heads and part of the tails of comets.

Ion An atom that has an electrical charge because of the loss or gain of one or more electrons.

Jovian Planets Same as the major planets.

Major Planets Jupiter, Saturn, Uranus, and Neptune; sometimes Pluto is included. Also called Jovian planets.

Meteor A small object from outer space that produces a streak of light as it enters the earth's atmosphere.

Meteor Shower Large numbers of meteors that appear to come from a single point; caused when earth collides with a swarm of meteor particles.

Meteorics The science of meteors, meteorites and meteoroids.

Meteorite A meteor that falls to the surface of the earth.

Meteoriticist A scientist who studies meteors, meteorites and meteoroids.

Meteoroid The solid object in space before it enters the earth's atmosphere and becomes a meteor.

Micrometeor A tiny meteor of microscopic size.

Minor Planet Another name for asteroid.

Molecule A combination of two or more atoms that are bound together.

Nucleus (of a comet)   The solid center of a comet made up of bits of rock and metal frozen into a ball of ice.

Occultation   Blocking the light from a star or planet by another object in space.

Orbit   The path followed by a body around another body or point.

Perihelion   The point in an orbit closest to the sun.

Period   An interval of time, such as that required for a body in space to complete an orbit.

Planet   Any large body that moves in orbit around a central star.

Planetoid   Another word for asteroid.

Radiant   The point in the sky from which a meteor shower appears to come.

Shooting Star   Popular name for a meteor.

Spectroscope   A scientific instrument that separates light into a rainbowlike spectrum of colors, which helps to identify the elements that make up the source of light.

Star   An intensely hot sphere of gas that gives off heat and light.

Tail (of a comet)   A long trail of gases and dust from the head of a comet that always faces away from the sun; some comets have a gas tail and a separate dust tail.

Telescope   An optical instrument that helps people to see, measure, and photograph distant objects.

Terrestrial Planets   Mercury, Venus, Earth, and Mars. Also called earthlike planets.

TNT   Short for trinitrotoluene, a powerful explosive.

Index

The Author

Melvin Berger is a graduate of the University of Rochester and holds a master's degree from Columbia University. He did postgraduate work at the University of London. While in England, he developed a particular interest in modern astronomy. He has written more than sixty books for young readers, among them two companion volumes to *Comets, Meteors and Asteroids: Planets, Stars and Galaxies* and *Quasars, Pulsars and Black Holes in Space*. Eight of his books have been given the Outstanding Science Books for Children Award of the National Science Teachers Association and the Children's Book Council.